KABBALAH ON **pain**

Kabbalah Publishing is a registered DBA of Kabbalah Centre International, Inc.

For further information:

The Kabbalah Centre
155 E. 48th St., New York, NY 10017
1062 S. Robertson Blvd., Los Angeles, CA 90035

1.800.Kabbalah www.kabbalah.com

First Edition
July 2007
Printed in USA
ISBN10: 1-57189-571-X
ISBN13: 978-1-57189-571-4

Design: HL Design (Hyun Min Lee) www.hldesignco.com

KABBALAH ON

pain

HOW TO USE IT TO LOSE IT

YEHUDA BERG

DEDICATION

To all those near and far who have felt the ache of the Rav's absence, to those who have felt the pain of loss that is so debilitating you think you can not go on . . . until from somewhere you find the strength to put one foot in front of the other and embrace the process . . . then the bitter turns slowly to sweet, and you discover that all along it was the Light in the center of the darkness.

TABLE OF CONTENTS

www.72.com

ACKNOWLEDGMENTS

To the people who make my life better each and every day—my parents, the Rav and Karen, my brother Michael, my wife Michal and our children—and to those who are such an important part of revealing this wisdom through their gifts and support: Billy Phillips, Stephanie Schottel, Peter Guzzardi, Hyun Min Lee, and Phyllis Henrici. Thank you all.

Chapter One

defining pain

Pain. We do everything in our power to numb or sup-
press it. When we can't, we use it to justify inflicting
pain on others, or to garner pity. Left unchecked, it can
tear us apart. Put to good use, it can bring us together.
More often than not, we allow it to make us feel isolated and alone.

What is pain?

I am not talking about the pain you feel when you stub
your toe or even when you experience serious bodily
injury or disease; this book isn't about physical pain. I
am talking about the other kind of pain—the type of
pain that rips us open emotionally, leaving us feeling
raw, vulnerable, and desperate.

You know the pain I am talking about.

On good days, the pain we experience is mere discomfort. On bad days, it is sheer agony. When it involves
love or loss, we call it heartbreak. Pain can take the
form of sadness, bitterness, or anxiety. The vast number

of variations on pain brings us to one conclusion: pain is personal, which means it manifests itself differently for everyone. My pain doesn't feel exactly the same way your pain does, and vice versa.

But no matter how much pain you have experienced in your life, here's something about pain you probably don't know: there are really only two types of pain. Just two. Temporary pain and deep pain.

The first type of pain is what we experience when our ego has been bruised or battered. It's the pain of embarrassment, humiliation, or shame. It's the punch to the gut you feel when someone hurts your feelings or a boss dwells on a mistake you made on a project you've been laboring over. It's the slow burn you feel when you just aren't getting what you feel should be coming to you, or you're being judged for a comment you didn't even make, a crime you didn't commit, or a characteristic you don't possess.

We all know the heady exhilaration we feel when someone compliments our appearance or praises us for a
job well done. The type of pain I'm talking about here
is the flip side of flattery. Its bite can feel like a stab to
the solar plexus, but this type of pain always dissipates.
It comes and it goes. It's temporary.

In the 19th century, a kabbalist named Kotzker Rebbe
was known for doling out this brand of short-lived pain.
His life consisted of two things: praying and tearing
apart his students' egos. This brilliant man would
berate his students. He had the gift of finding and
exposing a person's weaknesses, laying them bare for
all to see. To be around him was extremely painful,
because there was nowhere to hide from his blinding
light.

Yes, being around him was *painful*—the profound discomfort you feel when someone tells you what he or
she really thinks and, in that moment, every fiber of
your body wishes the floor would swallow you whole.

This kind of pain may seem like just a necessary evil, but it can actually have substantial benefits. Yes, I know this may be a tough sell, but we'll talk more about why this type of pain is really a good thing despite its short-term sting. We'll discover why pain to the ego paves the way for lasting satisfaction and peace.

But before we get there, it's time to introduce you to the other type of pain. This pain is the real deal. It is the kind of pain that affects us at the level of the soul.

Although now we are talking about profound suffering, this pain too has a decidedly silver lining. In fact, it has the power to take you to your next level of consciousness—if you recognize the opportunity embedded in the pain. Examples of life-altering pain include losing a loved one, surviving a terrible trauma, or losing everything in a natural disaster. Surely this must be the kind of pain we could do without. But once again, Kabbalah takes what seems obvious and turns it on its head. In this case Kabbalah tells us that without pain at the level of the soul we'd lose the one thing that gives life meaning: the opportunity to change.

Yes, change. Growth. Transformation.

This means that huge rewards are built into this second type of pain. It's akin to the experience of giving birth. Without the pain a mother endures, there would be no life at all. This pain is necessary and its gift is awe-inspiring.

In fact, in order to bring anything of lasting value into this world, we *must* experience soul-level pain. Pain and joy are two faces of the same coin. The *Zohar*, Kabbalah's central text, tells the story of Rav Shimon Bar Yochai. Rav Shimon lived in Israel during the second century, during the Roman occupation, a time of great intolerance and bloodshed. The Romans executed Rav Shimon's teacher, the great Rav Akiva, because he refused to forsake his spiritual teaching. To avoid the same punishment, Rav Shimon ran into the mountains with only the rags on his back and took refuge in a secluded cave. Over the course of his thirteen years in isolation, the wisdom of the universe, Kabbalah, was revealed to him. When he finally stepped out of the cave, his physical appearance was almost painful to behold. His pale, gaunt body was covered with suppurating sores. But his spirits were high; he was joyous and fulfilled.

How could that be?

Because he had revealed the wisdom of Kabbalah, the entire *Zohar*, the sacred text of Kabbalah, during his long stay in the cave. Without Rav Shimon's physical sacrifice, he would not have been able to serve as the channel to bring the beauty and insight of Kabbalah to the world.

When we consider pain at the level of the soul—the deep-seated pain that Rav Shimon experienced—we are looking at the type of pain required in order to reveal large amounts of what kabbalists call Light. If you are familiar with Kabbalah, you've probably heard

this term before. If you have not, this book will introduce you to this infinite energy, whose sole purpose is
to fill you with a peace beyond anything you have ever
known.

But we don't have to go back centuries to see examples
of great kabbalists experiencing tremendous pain in
order to reveal this unimaginable, God-created peace
and joy. In the 20th century a great kabbalist and
scholar named Rav Yehuda Ashlag was responsible for
deciphering a wealth of vital, kabbalistic texts. He
passed these teachings on to Rav Yehuda Brandwein,
who then passed them on to my father, Kabbalist Rav
Berg. Each of these scholars suffered greatly at the
hands of those who believed that Kabbalah should be
accessible to only a handful of chosen students. Rav
Ashlag himself was badly beaten and left to die in a
pool of his own blood. My father was isolated by his
spiritual community to the point where he had difficulty supporting his family. My mother, Karen Berg, was
assaulted for her beliefs and ended up in the hospital.
My brother and I were refused entry to one school after

another. All this happened because people feared that, if this ancient wisdom fell into the wrong hands, it might be abused.

Instead, it has been the great kabbalistic leaders of every generation who have been abused. It was kabbalists like my mother, my father, and their teachers who suffered. But instead of allowing this physical and emotional pain to keep them from spreading their message, they used it to strengthen their resolve. In this book, you too will learn how to use your pain to your advantage and ultimately release its grip on you forever.

I wanted to write a book about freeing ourselves from pain and finding this lasting peace that we call Light. But I realized that, in order to do that, I would need to do something strange: I would need to talk about war. Why? Because in order to have peace, we must have war. That is the arrangement we chose for ourselves a very long time ago, but we'll get to that shortly.

I know that it's risky to discuss politics and war among friends. But that's what we are going to do. We're going to approach the topic of war head-on. Because the sooner we do, the sooner we can find eternal freedom from pain.

Chapter Two

war
(and peace)

There is only one war. Just one. Make no mistake. And it's a war that deserves every last ounce of our attention, effort, and time.

This war has only one enemy. Just one. Make no mistake. And this ruthless enemy has an endless supply of under-handed tricks and tactics.

Who it this enemy?

Let me tell you first who the enemy IS NOT.

The enemy is not a Muslim. The enemy is not a Jew. Nor a Christian, atheist, Buddhist, or a religious fanatic of any kind.

SO WHO ON EARTH IS THIS ENEMY?

You are.

And, actually, I am the enemy, too. We all are—not our physical bodies, or our races, or our religious beliefs, but rather a very particular part of our make-up. The enemy, you see, is a distinct aspect of our being, and it is the *only* enemy we have.

Its name is ego.

Rest assured that ego will get plenty of our attention in later chapters. For now, it's important to understand that this enemy, this calculating foe, has blinded us. Completely. And because this enemy has blinded us, we experience no end of pain in our lives. And it gets worse. We have been masterfully tricked into waging war against our fellow man instead of battling the true enemy—ego.

And wage war we do—on many levels. We wage war against our families, our co-workers, and our neigh-bors. We wage war on global battlefields—against peo-ple we do not even know.

Just as you've begun thinking this deception couldn't get any worse, I'm here to tell you that it has. This enemy, our ego, has succeeded in doing the impossible. It has gone so far as to trick us into providing it shelter. The ego has manipulated us into protecting it, and we do. Time and time again. We protect the one, true enemy that wants to keep us from true happiness. Against an enemy like this, we are going to have to pull out all the stops.

Yes, there is a war to be waged if we want to be free of suffering and filled with lasting peace—it just might not be what you had envisioned. It's not the bloody warfare we see raging on our televisions; it's a quieter, more insidious war—which makes it even more challenging to win. But if you picked up this book, my bet is that you're up for the challenge.

What does all of this mean? This means that war itself is not inherently terrible. Some wars are worth fighting—the war against the ego is one such war. In fact, it is the war to end all wars, once and for all, that will create never-ending harmony for all peoples, nations, and faiths.

THE GOOD WAR

Contrary to popular belief, war is not a bad thing. What's bad is when you fight the wrong war. Wrong wars are made up of bloody battles that result in short-lived peace, at best, and continued chaos at worst. The wrong wars benefit no one, and the pain they inflict is pointless. The lives of those entangled in battle become a wasteland of incessant hurt and heartache.

Are you depressed yet? Don't be. If you choose to use the kabbalistic tools provided in this book, you can learn to fight the right war—against the real enemy—so you will never have to suffer again. In fact, not only will you not suffer, you will experience fulfillment above and beyond anything you have ever known in this lifetime.

You might be wondering by now: Why does the pain of war have to exist in the first place? Who's the genius that came up with the concepts of war and pain?

THE MEANING OF LIFE

You are not the first to contemplate questions like these. People have wondered about the reason for pain and war throughout the ages. Kabbalah provides simple yet penetrating insights into why they exist—more importantly, why we exist.

If you are already familiar with Kabbalah, you know I have written many books on the subject. But there's one analogy I like to offer students that brings them to the "ah-ha!" moment quickly and you don't have to read a library of books to get there.

Tooth Decay

Have you ever had an awful toothache? *Remember your discomfort. Recall the fear of going to the dentist. Remind yourself of the needle that shot Novocain into your gums. Evoke the unsettling sound of the drill.*

The pain of a severe toothache coupled with an hour in the dentist's chair is not a pleasant experience. With that in mind, I'll ask you this:

IS IT SAFE TO SAY THAT YOU POSSESS WITHIN YOU
A DESIRE TO NOT EXPERIENCE AN EXCRUCIATING
TOOTHACHE?

I think it's accurate to suggest that all of us have this
same desire.

But now answer this next question:

WERE YOU AT ALL AWARE OF THIS DESIRE <u>BEFORE</u>
I ASKED THE QUESTION?

Your answer is most likely no. Odds are, you weren't
thinking about your desire to not have a toothache
before I brought up the subject. You were not consciously experiencing the fulfillment and the peace of
mind that goes with having a mouth free of pain. Do
you know why? This particular desire was *already* satisfied. You didn't have a toothache, and thus your desire

to not have a toothache was fulfilled 100%. This is why you were not even aware of it.

But if you had an unbearable toothache right now, you would certainly be aware of your desire to not have one. The *desire* to not experience the pain would awaken very quickly. Likewise, when the dentist fixes the tooth and the pain disappears, your joy and gratitude for being pain-free would be immense, although it also would be short-lived.

UNAWARE AT BIRTH

Are you starting to catch on? Now keep this analogy in mind while I take it one step further. You see, in the beginning we were all unaware, too.

According to Kabbalah, when the souls of humanity were originally created, the Creator filled us with endless happiness of every kind. Kabbalists call this infinite fulfillment Light. But we were not aware, conscious, or appreciative of this Light. Why? Because the instant we were created we were immediately brimming with the stuff. We were born completely satisfied. Every desire was fulfilled beyond measure; that was all we knew. And since we knew nothing but this divine fulfillment, it was as if we were asleep, unconscious, and unappreciative of what we were receiving—just as you were unaware a moment ago of the joy and fulfillment that you were enjoying by not having a toothache.

The souls of humanity were oblivious at birth, so we were unable to fully grasp and enjoy the happiness that we were receiving.

Please understand that the creation of our souls, our consciousness, our true self, took place long before this physical world came into existence. So when I talk about the creation of the souls of humanity, I am referring directly to a spiritual reality that existed before the physical universe was created, a reality far more authentic and real than the material world around us.

THE PAIN OF EXISTENCE

You and I, and all the souls of humanity literally asked our Creator to place us in a world of pain and suffering. We made this request in order to awaken our desire for the Light of the Creator, the source of our fulfillment, so that we could appreciate and enjoy everything that was given to us.

That's it. That's the reason for the trees, the mountains, the sun, the planets, the atoms, the birds, the rivers, and most importantly, for your existence!

Okay. I know what you are thinking: Who in their right mind would want to experience the bloodshed, abuse, and pain that has accompanied every generation of souls over the last few millennia? And how could God listen and place us in such a heartless world of excruciating pain simply because we wanted to appreciate and desire the free gifts that God gave us?

Two excellent questions. The excellent answer begins
in our next chapter.

Chapter Three

pain has a
purpose

The Creator did *not* want to see us suffer. Not for a minute. Not for a second. We asked for it. If you think about it, it makes perfect sense. How can one genuinely experience true happiness if one has no appreciation of it? In other words, it's darkness that gives definition and existence to light. We know and appreciate things only by their opposite. So the souls of humanity asked the Creator to provide a path of pain in order to ignite a true desire for happiness and a genuine appreciation for the fulfillment that God wanted to give us.

Imagine a cold glass of lemonade. You could not fully appreciate this cold glass of lemonade if you had just finishing drinking a gallon of ice water, right? If you're not thirsty, you won't enjoy drinking. If, however, you wandered through a blistering hot, bone-dry desert for a few days, you most definitely would appreciate that tall, cool glass of sparkling lemonade.

That's why this world of pain was created. We wanted to become thirsty for the Light in order to genuinely enjoy drinking the fulfillment that flowed from the

Creator. This earth, our physical existence, is the desert through which we journey in order to stimulate this great thirst. Our world of darkness makes us crave the Light of the Creator. Now what does this mean more specifically?

THE WAY OF OUR WORLD

The fulfillment God originally gave us included immortality. Yes, when the souls of humanity were created, we could live forever. But we asked to experience death. Why? Because only death could make us thirsty for life, much the way only sadness could make us thirsty for joy.

God also gave us genuine well-being. As a result, we asked to experience sickness and disease. Only illness would make us thirsty for health and healing.

And the Creator gave us complete wisdom and truth. Therefore we sought to experience a world of utter ignorance, superstition, and lies.

God initially gave us all the answers to life. Then we asked God to allow us to experience a world of unending questions, in order to become truly thirsty for answers.

Get the drift?

We wanted to arouse a great thirst, a massive hunger, and a limitless desire for everything that God was giving freely to us. We wanted to wake up from our slumber. We wanted to become truly alive and appreciative of everything that was being handed to us. The only way to truly develop this profound awareness and gratitude was to experience its opposite. You always crave precisely what you can't have, right? It makes perfect sense.

And here's where it all comes together: the world we have chosen to live in is the exact opposite of true reality—the reality in which we were originally created. And this is why there is so much pain in the world.

Here's another way of phrasing this ultimate truth: originally God gave us Himself—the ultimate source of all possibility and goodness. We asked to experience a world without God, a world where the one true Creator was hidden. Look around. This is why people all around the world ask every day: "Where is God when I need Him most?" You've heard yourself ask the question, "How can God allow all of this suffering to happen?" This is why there are so many different definitions and ideas about the force we call God. And this is why there has been so much blood spilled in search of the one, true God.

And you know what else?

It didn't have to be this way. I repeat: it did **not** have to be this way. And it definitely doesn't have to **stay** this way. We all have within us the ability to end the pain in this world by bringing God into our lives. This can happen for all people and for all faiths.

And this is precisely what God has always wanted for us.

THE DIVINE STAND-IN

God could not—and did not—sit back and just watch us suffer, even though we needed it, even though we asked for it. Think about this for a moment. God must be pretty smart. After all, He is the source of all knowledge and all solutions. So God should be able to figure out a way in which we human beings can appreciate His goodness **without** having to go through all of this torture and torment. If anyone could do it, God should be able to solve this riddle.

And he did.

God came up with a brilliant idea—utterly genius! God developed a strategy that would allow a stand-in to experience pain on our behalf, so that we could spend our time and efforts receiving infinite fulfillment instead.

Yes, God created the ultimate proxy, the perfect substitute for you and me, so our souls would not have to endure the pain of embarrassment, humiliation, shame, heartache, and all of the other suffering that comes with physical existence.

In an action movie, the star of the film usually doesn't perform his or her own stunts, right? A stunt double assumes all the risk, injury, and pain. It's the same idea here: God created the ideal stunt double to carry the burden of pain on our behalf, so that while the stunt double was busy feeling our pain, we could connect to the Light, the source of all bliss and the polar **opposite** of the worst pain imaginable!

So what happened? What's the problem? Why do we all have pain in our lives? The problem is this: we keep getting in the way! We keep inadvertently pushing the stunt double aside. Why? 99% of us don't even know that a stunt double exists! But this stunt double is the key to finding peace.

Now, this might come as a surprise, but this stunt double is really our ego. Yes, the same ego—the same ENEMY—we talked about before.

That means our goal is to make sure that this stunt double, our ego, takes on all of our pain—every last bit of it. Sometimes we might wish that our ego could find another job and take the high road out of town, but while we are living on Earth, our ego is here to stay. (Soon we will discuss why that is a good thing.)

So, what exactly do I mean when I say that we want our ego to take on all of our pain? What does that look like in everyday life? We'll explore the specifics in a later chapter, but here's the gist of it.

Your friend makes a comment about how he could never juggle graduate school and a full-time job like you are doing, because he couldn't neglect his family like that. Ouch! That hurt (your ego, that is). And that's OKAY. That's what your ego is there for—to take the blow. What your ego heard was that you must be a negligent parent for trying to earn a paycheck and fulfill your dream of going to graduate school at the same time. Your ego wants you to respond with a fiery retort about your friend's less-than-stellar parenting skills.

But you don't have to. The moment you recognize that it's your ego that's taken the hit, and not your soul (your true authentic self), you no longer have to take his comments so personally. You cease having to REACT to your friend. You can let ego-bruising comments be just that: ego-bruising, and not soul-crushing. And, again, that's what your ego is designed to do: to be battered and bruised. You—your soul, that is—is designed to receive nothing but joy and fulfillment. Let your ego take the knocks, while you connect to the Light by NOT reacting.

Does this mean that while our ego is being pummeled, we try our best to override the bitterness and negativity that we feel? Not at all. In fact, bitterness and negativity don't even have to be part of the picture. How is this possible? It requires a tiny shift in consciousness or perspective, but it's a shift that each of us has the ability to make. If we see the hits as a pathway we must take in order to receive Light, then the hits cease to be a form of suffering; instead, they become blessings. They are like a good workout—strenuous and challenging but, in the end, undeniably worthwhile.

The following story illustrates this point well:

The Landowner and the Deputy

There was once a well-respected landowner who maintained a great deal of territory on behalf of the King. His business operations ran smoothly, and his dealings were always honorable. Much of his success he owed to a young man whom he employed to assist him. In fact, the young man was instrumental in the Landowner's business. Without his hard work, the Landowner would have been left in a lurch on many occasions. Despite the trust that the Landowner had in the young man, when the Landowner was called away on business, he assigned his Deputy to oversee the land, and he instructed the Deputy to take good care of the young man, who would some day become the Landlord's trusted advisor.

It didn't take long for the Deputy to see how practical, honest, and wise the young man

*was, and this deeply threatened the greedy
Deputy, who hoped to squelch the young man's
influence over the Landowner. With this in
mind, the Deputy concocted a plan in which it
would appear as though the young man had
made a critical mistake in his work. The very
next day, upon discovering the young man's
accounting "error," the Deputy lashed him
without mercy and sent him on his way.*

*The young man arrived home crying, and his
wife rushed to him with grave concern. She
had never seen her kind husband so troubled.
"Why are you crying?" She asked. "I was
lashed today for a mistake that I did not make,"
he replied. "Have no worries," she responded
knowingly, "the moment the Landowner
returns, you will be compensated for the cruel-
ty that you have endured. The Landowner is a
kind and generous man who will recognize the
Deputy's malice."*

His wife's response provided the weary man solace. He had always worked hard for the Landowner and had enjoyed the kindness that he had received in return. The arrival of the Deputy had been expected; his abuse, however, had not. For days, the young man endured agonizing lashes across his wounded back, leaving his body and his resolve battered and bruised upon the Landowner's return.

The young man knew that the story of the Deputy's conniving ways would be difficult to believe. Moreover, his accusations could result in more pain or death if the Landowner chose not to believe him. Despite his fear, he remembered his wife's words and confronted the Landowner and explained the Deputy's beatings. The Landowner looked into the eyes of the trusted young man and saw the sincerity that he recognized so well. The man had suffered a great deal, and the Landowner could see the vulnerability and fear in his friend's face.

Without a moment's hesitation he asked, "How many lashes did you receive from the Deputy?" "Nine," replied the young man solemnly.

The Landowner looked at the Deputy and said, "For the pain that you inflicted, give the young man a gold coin." The Deputy took out a gold coin and hesitated to give it to the young man. "No," said the Landowner, "let him receive a gold coin for EVERY lash he received from you." The Deputy counted out nine gold coins and reluctantly handed them to the young man.

The young man thanked the Landowner profusely and ran home to his wife. The door swung open, and his wife looked up to find her husband crying and clutching something in his hand. "What happened? Why are you crying?" she asked, afraid that her direction may have caused her husband greater suffering. "You were right," he explained, "the Landowner had

me generously compensated for my suffering. He had the Deputy give me one gold coin for every lash of the Deputy's whip."

"Then, my word, but why are you crying?" she asked. "Because I only received nine lashes," he exclaimed.

Once the young man knew the benefit he would receive for the lashes he had been given, the lashes themselves no longer caused the young man suffering. In fact, he wanted to receive even more! The same is true for our ego. If we truly understand that every time we allow the ego to feel discomfort and pain that we will be compensated handsomely, we will no longer view the pain to our ego as a form of suffering. This is because we will recognize the discomfort as a direct route to satisfaction and joy.

I'm not advocating that you allow yourself to be beaten at the hands of some evil person. That's not the point of the story, and I think that you know that. This story, this metaphor, is a window through which you can see the happy ending that comes after you have stayed the course by allowing your ego to take a few lashes along the way. This story can become your story if gold, in the form of Light, is what you seek.

WHAT'S IN A NAME?

That which we call a rose by any other name would smell as sweet.
    —William Shakespeare

The ego has many names, but no matter how you slice it, it's still the ego. It's still the voice that lures us away from the Light—if we choose to let it. So you can call it your:

STUNT DOUBLE
STAND-IN
ULTIMATE PROXY
ENEMY

There's even another name we haven't discussed yet. Are you curious to know the other name of this powerful force? He goes by the name of Satan.

THE TRUTH ABOUT THE DEVIL

As crazy as it may sound, the devil is actually a pretty noble fellow. Allow me to explain by sharing a simple story from the *Zohar*.

The Prince And The Prostitute

Once there was a great king who possessed a profound and undying love for the subjects of his kingdom. He was a king in every sense of the word. He was compassionate, brave, and profoundly humble. The king felt honored and privileged to serve and care for his people. And he did so with a loving, just, and sympathetic heart. His subjects returned this love and loyalty in equal measure. Thus, they were heartbroken when they discovered that the king had decided it was time to abdicate his throne and pass the crown on to his only son.

The king was a special man who possessed enough warmth to love his son and all of his

subjects equally. And it was imperative to His Majesty that his son be able to offer the same love and loyalty to the subjects of the kingdom.

Before he could hand over the crown, throne, and treasures of the kingdom to his son in good conscience, the king knew his son must first demonstrate character, integrity, profound love, and loyalty. If he could do so, the prince could definitely become a king who was loving and loyal to his subjects. And so the king decided to test the young man. He asked him to perform a special task as proof of his love and loyalty. The king asked his son to refrain from temptations that would compromise his character and integrity. The prince agreed. Days later, the king sent his son to another village to conduct some business on behalf of the king. After the prince departed, the king summoned the most beautiful and seductive prostitute in his kingdom. The king asked her for a special favor that would inevitably benefit all the people. The prostitute should employ all of her sexual charm and charisma to lure the prince into her bedroom. She agreed.

The prostitute traveled to the same village as the prince and began to work her magic upon him. She was loving and sensual, and the prince was ready to take her when he suddenly remembered his promise to his father. Mustering all of his self-control and willpower, the prince declined the advances of the prostitute. It wasn't easy, but he succeeded. When the prostitute reported back to the king, he was overjoyed. Comforted by the knowledge that his son possessed all the qualities necessary to resist temporary temptation and truly care for his subjects, the king proudly bestowed the crown and all of the treasures of the kingdom to his son.

That is how the story ends. But the *Zohar* asks an important question: Who is ultimately responsible for the prince acquiring the crown and the treasures of the kingdom?

The answer: the prostitute!

Without her involvement, the son would never have been able to prove himself worthy of the throne.

This simple story gives us some insight into the benefits that can derive from the works of the so-called devil. To begin with, the correct term for "him" is actually *Adversary*. *Adversary* is the correct English translation of the Hebrew word Satan. It does not mean devil or demon. The first time the word Satan appears is in the Hebrew Bible, dating back some 3400 years!

The force that we all call Satan is a legitimate adversarial force. It is a distinct entity that seeks to help us for the benefit of ourselves, just like the prostitute assisted the king for the benefit of the kingdom. This Adversary's purpose is to take on the pain and suffering of the world on our behalf—*if we allow him to.*

But we don't.

That's because he can be quite hard to locate.

If we cannot locate him, how are we supposed to hand over to him all of our pain and sorrow?

We have to learn to recognize his calling card.

Chapter Four
the choice

I don't give them hell. I just tell them the truth and they think it's hell.

—US President Harry Truman

The Adversary, Satan, is the human ego. Yes, the ego is the one who:

- Sends messages to you saying that you are separate from everyone else.
- Fills your mind with painful, negative thoughts.
- Encourages you to protect it at all costs.

The ego works awfully hard to persuade you that it is your true self, your divine nature. It's not. However, as human beings, we come equipped with a built-in receiver tuned in to the messages the ego sends our way.

But you are not your ego.

You might think you are one and the same, but therein lies the problem. And that's why you continue

KABBALAH ON **pain**

to experience psychic pain. The good news is that as soon as you detach yourself from your ego, you begin to detach yourself from pain.

To your credit, there is a very good reason that you think you and the ego are one and the same. The ego can be very seductive. Think back on our story about the Prince and the Prostitute. The king did not send an unappealing harlot to seduce his son. On the contrary, the king sent the most bewitchingly beautiful prostitute in the kingdom. A test must be difficult if it's going to be a true test. And that's exactly what this game we play with the ego is all about. It's a test with amazing rewards if we choose to pass it.

Just like the king's son who refused to succumb to the prostitute's advances and inherited a kingdom for his efforts, we can earn everlasting fulfillment and peace by taking the path of most resistance. That means instead of taking the easy way out and experiencing temporary pleasure (like the son would have experienced had he slept with the prostitute), we recognize such temptations for exactly what they are—the ego at work. And we move past them.

By *not* falling for the short-term pleasure, by *not* succumbing to ego, we allow it to take on our pain. It pouts and complains that it didn't get what it wanted. It wallows in suffering and self-pity, but we don't. Our soul remains free—free to soak up the real pleasure, the long-lasting satisfaction that only the Light of the Creator can provide.

This deserves repeating. The Adversary, the ego, is here to take pain for you, *if* you put him in pain's way.

He is called an Adversary for a good reason. He tests you. He tirelessly works to find ways to trick you into taking the pain so he doesn't have to. How? The Adversary constantly deceives you into believing that the ego is your true identity. Remember, he does this by sending negative thoughts racing through your mind, prompting you to say hurtful things to others, or causing you to feel angry when you don't get what you think you deserve.

But we know that these thoughts and inclinations are not part of your true, loving nature. How do we know this? Just remember where you came from—you came from a loving source absolutely free of judgment, pain, sadness, and anger. So these thoughts and inclinations can't be yours. They can only belong to Satan.

Embedding mistaken beliefs in your mind is an integral part of the Adversary's war strategy. His battle plan depends on it. But you don't have to fall for it anymore. You no longer have to protect, defend, and nurture the ego at all costs. There is another way—a way that starts with identifying the true enemy. Follow this path, and it will lead you to a pain-free existence.

This is your choice to make. And never forget, you ALWAYS have a choice.

THE CHOICE

We discovered earlier that the souls of humanity asked to be placed in a world that was the opposite of true reality.

Let's revisit this critical idea and pare it down to its essentials:

- True Reality contained unending happiness.
- We asked to experience sadness.

- True Reality consisted of immeasurable joy.
- We asked to experience pain.

- True Reality consisted of lasting peace.
- We asked for a world in which we could battle and win the constant war.

- True Reality included immortality.
- We asked to experience a world that included death.

Despite this arrangement, we still have a vital choice to make every time we confront the ego (which happens continually). Follow this carefully, because it all comes down to this. All of life is explained and understood right here, right now. Ready? Here we go.

The Choice:

- **Your ego experiences sadness on your behalf—*or you do.***

- **Your ego experiences pain on your behalf —*or you do.***

- **You wage constant war upon your ego—*or you wage constant war against your fellow man and he wages war against you.***

- **Your ego experiences death on your behalf— *or you do.***

When you choose to protect your ego, your body and soul will experience pain. When you allow your ego to take on the pain, your body and soul will experience contentment.

That's it. That's life. That's the way it is.

I know—*it can't be that simple.* That's your ego talking. The Adversary would rather you believe that life is complex and conditional. Why? True reality is simple and trouble-free. And the Adversary is giving you the opposite picture of reality.

So why do you do it? Why do you allow your ego to run your life and bring more misery to your existence? Why don't we all recognize the ego as our true enemy? Why don't we figure out that the ego is not really who we are?

There is only one answer: PAIN!

Chapter Five

pleasure
vs. pain

Remember that I said in the beginning of this book that there are two kinds of pain.

They are:

1. Pain in our ego, which lasts but a short while.
2. Pain in our body and soul, which lasts a lifetime.

There are also two forms of pleasure. They are:

1. Pleasure for our ego, which lasts but a short while.
2. Pleasure for our body and soul, which lasts a lifetime.

Every time we gratify the ego by giving in to its promptings, we receive a quick injection of pleasure. And humankind is addicted to pleasure. Do you know why? Pleasure is true reality! Pleasure is why we were created in the first place. Pleasure is our true home, our true origin. But the kind our ego gives us is not the kind of pleasure that abides. Not only is it temporary, it's also followed by long-term pain for our body and soul. So it contains a double whammy.

Think of a time when you were feeling worn out, depleted of energy. Maybe your spouse or your child reached out to you; he or she needed your love or attention. But all you could think was, "Here is one more person who needs something from me. I give and I give and I give. Why is it never enough?" And before you even had a moment to resist these ego-inspired thoughts, you responded to your loved one's request with a caustic comment or refusal. And there is no doubt that the momentary release of negative energy you experienced was satisfying. It brought you pleasure. But do you remember how short-lived it was?

Before you even had a moment to revel in it, pain moved in to replace the pleasure. Not only did you see the pain you inflicted in the crestfallen face of your spouse or child, you felt the pain yourself. You were disappointed in your behavior, frustrated by the situation, and suddenly felt crummy overall. You hurt your loved one; you hurt yourself. Chalk up one more win for the ego.

Now what would have happened had you recognized that moment for what it truly was—your ego's attempt to keep you isolated from the love and the Light of others? What would have happened had you reached out for your loved one in spite of the ego's negative incoming broadcasts? Let me tell you.

You would have experienced momentary egocentric pain. It would have felt very difficult—incredibly uncomfortable—to reach out at that moment. And if you were really out of practice at allowing yourself to love and be loved, it might have felt like a punch in the arm. That's because overriding the ego is always painful.

But here's where the magic comes in.

The discomfort that you feel when you honor your soul and allow your ego to take the hit is immediately replaced by immeasurable joy (the kind that comes straight from the Creator). Not only do you feel joy within, you can literally see joy revealed in the face of your child or your partner the moment you give of yourself. This is the reason we must fight for this divine peace. The temporary discomfort—the momentary pain—that you feel is necessary in order to nurture the soul and reveal Light in this world. Leave the ego, Satan, to deal with the pain.

It sounds relatively simple: let the ego take the fall, and you'll feel lasting joy.

So what's the problem?

SIMPLE, BUT NOT EASY

It's rarely an easy thing to do. We are drawn to pleasure, remember? Most of us choose pleasure over pain any day of the week—temporary or otherwise. But remember, you're not the one really making that choice. You're allowing your ego to do the choosing for you. And the Adversary pulls no punches. He doesn't hold back. He uses every trick in the book to tempt you, to test you, to challenge you, and to trick you.

If you need proof, think of all of the bloodshed that has taken place since the dawn of recorded time. The truth is that the Adversary, the ego, will go so far as to encourage murder just to protect itself. We can make the choice to do the exact opposite by resisting these negative temptations and massacring the ego instead! When everyone chooses to demolish the ego, the physical and mental pain caused by conflict will disappear forever.

Remember, infinite fulfillment has its opposite—infinite evil. Look around. We see infinite evil on the news, in our neighborhoods, and all too often in our own hearts. When I say infinite evil, keep in mind that disgracing someone in public is just as evil as murder. Physical abuse harms the body whereas spiritual abuse, such as humiliation, harms a person's soul. Think about it. You can spill someone's blood with a knife, but it can be even more painful to embarrass him or her, causing that person immense shame and sending blood rushing to his or her face in humiliation.

The Adversary will motivate you to hurt others, just to keep himself from being hurt. The Adversary is in constant defense mode. He will trigger tremendous pain the moment you even consider threatening the ego. On the flip side, the Adversary will ignite enormous pleasure when you protect and serve the ego. Yes, it's true that our instinct is to choose pleasure over pain. But this instinctual response is based on a critical lack of information.

THE SECRET YOU NEVER KNEW

The key piece of information that we are missing is this:

> There is far more pleasure to be had if we just
> choose MOMENTARY pain.

We think we are being greedy when we choose a short-term shot of pleasure, but in fact we are not being greedy enough! We are selling ourselves short—time and time again. We have access to limitless fulfillment. It is ours for the taking! But we continue to make this lousy trade-off because we fail to see beyond the initial pain. And that's how the Adversary dupes us. He tries to keep us from seeing the long-term benefit of choosing the pain that comes from warring against the ego. He only shows us the immediate picture. And the immediate picture looks pretty frightening—on the surface. But beneath it lies an infinite sea of contentment and joy.

THE ULTIMATE BATTLE

This divine contentment is, without a doubt, worth fighting for—even if it hurts. And the truth is that fighting is nothing new for you. You have been engaged in various struggles your whole life. You have been battling for financial security, happiness, love, and good health. But these are external battles. External battles never win the ultimate war. Never!

But you are in the process of learning what will. Remember that the most important war of all is an internal one against an insidious enemy that is just as real as those people who seem to wish you harm. And if you fight this war correctly, not only will your body and soul remain unharmed; if you learn to fight correctly, your body and soul will experience profound satisfaction and joy.

But have no worries. You won't be fighting this battle alone, and you will receive the finest training in the form of Kabbalah. You'll be receiving constant on-the-job experience.

When you're ready, you'll learn how you can use your enemy—your ego—to your ultimate advantage. Every time you do, you will be helping to create the perfect environment for sustainable, divine, peace on Earth—free of pain and suffering for all.

Chapter Six

an elite team

As you know, in all physical wars, there are many divisions in which you can fight. You can join the navy, army, marines, or air force. The collective goal of this military apparatus never wavers; it is to conduct an effective war and achieve victory against the perceived enemy. But you and I both know that achieving victory in a war in which blood is spilled is no victory at all. Victory, in this sense, is a complete misnomer.

That's because real victory can only be achieved within the context of the internal war we fight—the war against the ego. In this war, real peace—real victory—comes when we identify the true enemy, take a stand against its ploys, and elect to reveal light instead. When we take this route, we are guaranteed to avoid soul-crushing pain, while bringing forth unimaginable peace, love, and joy!

SPECIAL FORCES

Ultimately, this book is about joining an elite group that is specially trained to embrace temporary pain. This book is about coming head to head *on a daily basis* with the trickiest enemy known to man: the egocentric nature of humankind.

This means that the path of Kabbalah is the most difficult path in life, because you are forced to confront the enemy 24 hours a day, seven days a week, 365 days a year. We have a choice; as you know, we humans continuously pick up on the ego's broadcasts. So you'll be hearing the enemy's voice during every interaction with your loved ones, friends, and co-workers. When the stakes are highest, the ego is sure to be there.

There is no rest. There is no lull. There is no let-up.

I'll be honest. Most people who fight for the force that is Kabbalah go AWOL after a while. Why? The work is taxing, to say the least. Many people flee with fright the moment they catch their first glimpse of the real enemy. Why?

Because we love our ego.

Despite the pain and suffering it causes us, the ego disguises itself as our only source of pleasure. That's why the smallest amount of pain to our ego sends us running for cover. In the face of the ego, we completely forget about any divine payoff (in the form of Light) that we will receive and will *continue* to receive due to our courageous efforts.

As soon as the ego experiences a real battle for the first time, we are tempted to run and hide. Most people think they are tough, but the truth of the matter is that most of us are really not. Most of us are petrified when it comes to experiencing real war, and the small number of those willing to face the one true enemy reflects this fear. This is why humanity has been losing the war against the Adversary for the past several thousand years. We have been too terrified to fight the real internal war, so we have taken the easy route. We engaged in external wars instead, which has left us with nothing but a blood-soaked landscape.

THE FEAR OF PAIN

So now you know that the way of Kabbalah is tough. Real tough. But that's precisely why it has the power to reveal such unbelievable fulfillment. That's how it works.

The greater the challenge, the more potential for Light.

This means that the greater the pain and emotional turmoil that you feel in your life right now, the more potential you have to bring about peace, love, and joy in your life and the lives of those around you. But despite the guarantee of this divine compensation, it comes as no surprise that we tend to run in the exact opposite direction of adversity when we see it coming our way. We would do just about anything to keep our ego from being maimed in any way. In fact, most people would rather let their bodies bleed to death over a long period of time than experience a quick death of the ego.

You might think I am crazy, but history is proof. The evidence can be seen in thousands of years of human civilization. The ego has been running the show since the dawn of time. We die, we suffer, and we hurt because we are scared to death of ego pain. We refuse to surrender the ego and kill it once and for all. And right about now, the ego is most likely trying to convince you that what I am saying is absurd. But listen to your heart, for your heart recognizes truth when it hears it. In fact, if you are starting to get frightened, hurt, or shaken up even just a little bit, then you are finally starting to wake up to the critical task at hand.

As the saying goes, "no pain, no gain." I can't think of a more fitting motto than this one for the cause at hand. To gain advantage and to ultimately reveal Light in this war, you must endure pain. I know, I know—no one likes pain. But remember that ego pain is only temporary, no matter how its initial impact might feel. Nothing but the loving Light of the Creator lasts forever.

It's hard to convince people of this. Who in their right mind would embark on a path where pain in any form is guaranteed? Nobody—except the bravest of the brave. So in order to enlist men and women in this elite force, Kabbalah has a unique recruiting strategy.

It's called **The Burning Bush Recruitment Program**.

Chapter Seven

burn, baby, burn

You may have read the biblical story of Moses' encounter with the burning bush. If you're not familiar with the story, here's a brief synopsis. Moses comes across a burning bush while wandering in the desert. Remarkably, the bush does not disintegrate while burning. On the contrary, it's alive and well. The fire and the bush coexist simultaneously. Suddenly, Moses hears a voice emanating from the bush and it's calling out to him. Who is it? It's none other than God. God tells Moses to go into Egypt and free the Israelites who have been enslaved by Pharaoh for some 400 years. Moses agrees to do God's bidding.

Some 2000 years ago, the kabbalistic commentators revealed some remarkable insights into this story. They described the entire story as code. So let's take a moment to see how they deciphered the cryptic tale of the burning bush, including Moses' directive from God to free the people of Israel from slavery in Egypt.

CRACKING THE CODE

Code One

The story is *NOT* about Egypt. Egypt is a code word for the human ego. The Israelites were enslaved to their egos, *not to the Egyptians!* Pharaoh represents the DNA of the ego—its ultimate source.

By the way, this illustrates why some people might not want to look below the surface of a biblical story. For instance, as an Israelite, it's so much easier for me to point the finger of blame at Arabs, Egyptians and Muslims, especially when the Bible seems to back this up. Imagine how much more difficult it is for me to say the real enemy is actually my ego—myself and only myself! Now, that's not easy!

Code Two

According to Kabbalah, Egypt represents the material world, which caters to our ego in endless ways. This means that the exodus from Egypt is really about gaining freedom from our ego and achieving bliss in the physical world. It's about developing the know-how to reveal the Light that we each hold within ourselves, instead of relying on something external (like our possessions, relationships, and jobs) to bring us lasting happiness. Developing the skill to reveal Light is the path to true freedom. It's just like building a muscle. We challenge and strengthen ourselves, so that connecting to the Light gets easier and easier.

Code Three

The fire on the bush is the awesome energy that radiates from God, while the bush itself represents the physical world. Despite its unimaginable power and intensity, God's energy cannot destroy the physical world. This is why the bush does not turn to ash.

There's another telling insight that the ancient kabbalists reveal about the burning bush. Initially, Moses did not hear God's voice. Moses actually heard the voice of his own father calling him. Why? Kabbalah says that Moses needed to hear a voice that was friendly and familiar in order to draw him closer. Moses would have been too afraid if he knew who was really calling upon him. God's energy would have been too overwhelming for Moses, much the way we can become pretty freaked out when we think we are about to experience something that will deeply challenge us. But just as God understood what Moses needed to hear (and the voice he needed to hear it in), God knows what we need. Our Creator meets us where we are on our journey, making sure that the events and people in our lives (and even the unexpected voices!) are tailor-made for our spiritual growth.

THE LESSON OF THE BURNING BUSH

So why did I bring up the topic of the burning bush? There's an important lesson here that concerns the path of Kabbalah and, more specifically, the secret of the recruitment strategy I mentioned before.

At first, when we are introduced to kabbalistic wisdom, it's one big, warm, fuzzy experience. Everything sounds friendly, enlightening, thrilling, and exciting, because the deepest truths always feel familiar. Kabbalah's concepts resonate with our souls. It feels like we have known this stuff forever, and, in fact, Kabbalah helps us crystallize what we have understood subconsciously our whole lives. We are stimulated mentally, physically, spiritually. This happens in Kabbalah classes all over the world. All these good and familiar emotions draw us closer to the Light, closer to God, and closer to one another so that we will have the opportunity and desire to train intensely for the war of wars.

At first, there is no pain. There is no battle. Instead of hurting the ego, the ego is temporarily satiated with a morsel of pleasure in order to bring us closer. But the truth is this:

If we, like Moses, saw the real goal of Kabbalah from the get-go, we would be too scared to venture forward.

Now, don't get me wrong. The initial warm, fuzzy feeling is very real indeed, but it's also part of a recruiting strategy forged at the beginning of time. The familiar feeling that we have come home helps us to choose the difficult spiritual path, much the same way as an inspiring television commercial might do. When we first experience Kabbalah, we are given a measure of fulfillment to draw us into the path. Once we begin, the deeper training—the real work—becomes clearer.

I tell you this not to make you feel manipulated, but rather to prepare you for what inevitably comes when you engage in a battle. I tell you this so that you will start to see the ego as a tool you can use to reveal the Creator's Light from the inside out.

THE MINE FIELD

Once we set out on the path of warring against our true enemy, we get tested every step of the way. Something will invariably trigger an egocentric reaction within us, at which point we lose our cool, not to mention our motivation to continue. Often new recruits throw up their hands and simply walk away. This being said, in order to become a life-long warrior, we need to pass the pain of basic training—that initial pain that comes with having our ego poked, prodded, and provoked. These first tests are usually the toughest, because we are unaccustomed to recognizing the ego's underhanded maneuvers, let alone defending ourselves against them. Those first few times we often don't know what hit us. But these tests are preparing us to win the war.

Think about it. You've just begun your study of Kabbalah, and you're feeling pretty good, that is, until you encounter a driver with road rage on your way home from work, or your son tells you that he's been suspended from school. Or maybe your best friend beats you out for your dream job, or your wife tells you she's feeling unfulfilled in your marriage. Then what?

Your mind is suddenly flooded with various thoughts:

> *Kabbalah doesn't work.*
> *I'm out of here.*
> *It's the other person's fault.*
> *How could they do or say such a thing!*
> *God doesn't care.*
> *I am totally right and that person is totally wrong.*
> *If I don't give this person a piece of my mind, I'll feel worse.*
> *This is all such a waste of time.*
> *The teachings failed me.*
> *This is too difficult.*

Don't these sound like the complaints of recruits in basic training? It's right about here that many Kabbalah students lose it.

We shout when we could choose loving words.
We antagonize when we could just walk away.
We shut ourselves off when we could open
ourselves up.

These responses don't make us failures; we haven't totally blown it. We have to remember that we're human, and the messages we receive from the ego are as endless as the Light of the Creator. So when this happens to you, brush yourself off and try again. Trust me, you'll have plenty of opportunities to improve your skills by saying no to the ego and yes to loving words and thoughtful responses.

Even those of us who decide, "This war is not for me," will leave far better off than we were before. We will be departing basic training having gained a few new tools and some deeper insights about life, with a portion of our true being having been altered for the better. This positive energy will remain with us, because it comes from the Light and the Light is enduring in nature.

So what is there to lose?

Absolutely nothing . . . except an entire world of pain.

EVERY SOLDIER COUNTS

Despite the profound spiritual benefits of becoming a true warrior, and despite the promise that utilizing the wisdom of Kabbalah will eventually nullify pain forever, only a handful of people stick around to fight the real fight. Those who do join and remain (about 3% of all recruits) will achieve complete transformation. These people are called kabbalists. They are the great spiritual scholars of the past and present that you may have read about. A kabbalist's control over the ego is so unshakable that they are in complete alignment with God, which allows them control over their physical environment. Their mere presence brings great spiritual healing to those they encounter.

The other 97% of us might not achieve such transformation, but we are guaranteed to taste the rewards of our efforts. It's vital to note that it will be the contribution of *both*—the 97% who don't completely transform but fight every day to grow and change, and the 3% who earn the designation of kabbalist—that will help the world achieve the final victory.

Just like a colony of ants or a true community of individuals, every participant plays an important role. All contributions are important. Why? Because eventually we will reach a certain threshold, and once this critical mass is achieved, great transformations will take place. Together we will remove the ego from its self-appointed throne, and the war against the Adversary will be won.

It's entirely up to us to choose how hard we want to fight.

The 97% will be equipped to transform pain and suffering on their path to victory. But if you are a part of the 3%, the temporary pain that accompanies assault on the ego will give way to divine, uninterrupted fulfillment.

For those of us who want to bite the bullet and develop spiritually in this lifetime, our next chapter presents the tools and techniques for achieving personal victory.

And a personal victory for you has the power to lead to triumph for every soul on Earth.

Chapter Eight

victory

THE ANGEL OF DEATH

Most people don't even get to the burning bush stage. They never come across Kabbalah. They never even hear about this wisdom and technology. But you are reading this book, and that is no accident. You're tired of heartache and pain; you're tired of feeling battered and abused by life's whims. And, for perhaps the first time, you are open to another way—a way that puts you back in touch with all that is good and loving in this universe.

This concept might not sound controversial at first blush, but it is. In fact, Kabbalah has caused panic and opposition in various individuals for the last 2,000 years. Kabbalah has had many rabid opponents throughout history. They damned Kabbalah. They cursed it. They slandered it. They defamed it. They vilified it.

Now why would someone do such a thing?

On a subconscious, soul level these opponents knew what Kabbalah represented. It meant the end of all establishments whose power was founded on ego and self-interest. It meant the end of selfishness and self-indulgence. It meant the end of control over people and profiteering at the expense of others. Faced with such threats, the ego went wild.

Make no mistake. There is no other reason why people oppose Kabbalah. None. Kabbalah does not convert people. Kabbalah does not ask you to change your religion. It only asks that you defeat your ego so that you can share unconditionally with those around you. It enhances a person's existing beliefs and respect for those of others. It promotes unity, not separation. Inclusiveness, rather than exclusiveness. How? By providing each and every one of us with the necessary tools for achieving victory over our selfish inclinations.

Every other justification for opposing Kabbalah is nothing but an excuse provided by the ego. And the doubt you are feeling right now is also caused by your ego—

all of it, every ounce of skepticism and every trace of uncertainty!

The great kabbalists told us this war would be incredibly demanding. But they also said that where there is great challenge, there is great reward. In this case the reward is the end of death itself. That's right. Kabbalah promises us the end of death as the ultimate fruit of victory.

How could this be? Well, as it turns out, the ego and the Angel of Death are one entity.

Are you really that surprised?

A DROP OF POISON

Every ego-centered reaction brings a taste of death into our life. We consume a little bit of poison every time the ego motivates our behavior. Every time we lash out at a stranger or loved one. Every time we show intolerance for another race, gender, or religion. Every time we get defensive with a co-worker or boss. Every time we use our ego to cause pain instead of invite peace, we feed ourselves a bit of bitter-tasting death.

And when this poison finally reaches a critical level in our body, we die. We hit the tipping point. That's it. That's the only reason death takes place.

Imagine a lamp illuminating a room. If you drape a curtain over the lamp, the light in the room diminishes. Drape a second curtain over the lamp and the room is further darkened. If you keep draping curtains over the lamp, eventually the room will become pitch black. That is death. It's the point where the last flicker of light is blocked out.

Our soul is the lamp that keeps us alive. And every egocentric act is akin to drawing a curtain over the Light of
our soul. Each additional curtain dims our soul until we
reach that point where our body loses complete connection with the one true Source of everything.

Keep in mind the soul is still shining brilliantly, just as
the lamp continues to shine behind the curtain in the
dark room. It's only the layers of egocentric responses
that dim our life force. But the soul never dies. It shines
forever. Death occurs only when we block out the Light
of God completely.

THE EGO FIGHTS BACK

Now the ego will lead you to believe that we die because of our DNA, smoking, old age, disease, car accidents, and heart attacks. But this is simply not the case. In fact, Kabbalah says this is an absolute lie. These so-called causes are not the true cause. They are merely the physical manifestation of the true spiritual cause. This is important, so it bears repeating. Smoking, cancer, car accidents, heart attacks, strokes, and disease are only the mechanisms that are used once a certain threshold of death energy (ego) in our lives has been reached. I know this is difficult to accept and grasp. But just know that your difficulty in accepting these ideas is the war raging within you. You're knee-deep in battle right now. You are on the front lines. My only advice at this point is this: stay the course and fight back. You may have heard the term spiritual warfare before; now you're living it.

When you defeat your doubt and accept these kabbalistic truths about the ego 100%, you will win the war and achieve the death of death itself! It's been a long, hard-fought war for thousands of years. The war against death continues to this very day. Remember, not only is the ego the ultimate source of death, it is also the ultimate source of doubt!

What doubt?

All the doubt you feel right now about your ability to end death and the ego's ability to inflict it.

COURAGE VERSUS STUPIDITY

Stupidity, according to ancient kabbalists, is when a critic or detractor arbitrarily denounces, mocks, and derides ideas before ever giving the ideas a try. Kabbalah says be smart and courageous. How? By at least *considering* the promise of what this wisdom offers, and admit that you don't yet have the spiritual wisdom, maturity, and strength to fully understand its potential. It's okay to say "I don't know." There's nothing wrong with that. Healthy skepticism is welcome. But at least consider the possibility.

Most importantly, test it out. See if life changes when you fight the internal war. See if you witness miracles before your very eyes. If you don't, then quit. Stop fighting. Indulge the ego to your heart's content. But if you do see miracles, if you do experience positive change, you will know first-hand the power of this wisdom and the profound implications of becoming a true warrior. The proof lies in the living. There is no faith in Kabbalah; there are only results. I could tell you all day long that I live the miracle, but that would be a waste of my breath and your time if you didn't allow the miracle to unfold in your own life.

If you can at least consider the possibilities, you have courage, according to Kabbalah. And an ounce of courage is all you need to begin this journey.

SURVIVAL OF THE FITTEST

The survival instinct is the most powerful force on Earth, without question. And it's the ego that holds the trophy for the strongest survival instinct of all. The ego does not want to die. Why? Remember the stunt double metaphor from earlier? The ego—our stunt double—desperately wants to keep his job. He wants to keep us all disconnected from peace, love, and Light, so he can rule the roost. He wants to keep each of us full of pain, fear, and emotional turmoil. The ego would prefer you be the lamp in the corner covered with drapes of cloth, without even the tiniest bit of Light shining through. That's what the ego wants.

That's what the ego has always wanted, and it is willing to blind us with doubt in an attempt to desperately delay our progress and transformation. Just take a quick look at some of the ego's influence over the last 110 years:

Radio has no future.
—Lord Kelvin, 1897

That the automobile has practically reached the limit of its development is suggested by the fact that during the past year no improvements of a radical nature have been introduced.
—Scientific American, Jan. 2, 1909

Well informed people know it is impossible to transmit the voice over wires and that were it possible to do so, the thing would be of no practical value.
—Editorial in The Boston Post, 1865

What can be more palpably absurd than the prospect held out of locomotives traveling twice as fast as stagecoaches?
—The Quarterly Review, England,
  March 1825

While theoretically and technically television may be feasible, commercially and financially I consider it an impossibility, a development of which we need waste little time dreaming.
—Lee De Forest, American radio pioneer and inventor of the vacuum tube, 1926

We don't like their sound, and guitar music is on the way out anyway.
—President of Decca Records, rejecting The Beatles, 1962

To place a man in a multi-stage rocket and project him into the controlling gravitational field of the moon where the passengers can make scientific observations, perhaps land alive, and then return to Earth . . . I am bold enough to say that such a man-made voyage will never occur regardless of all future advances.
—Lee De Forest, 1957

A rocket will never be able to leave the Earth's atmosphere.
—The New York Times, 1936

Flight by machines heavier than air is unpractical and insignificant, if not utterly impossible.
—Simon Newcomb, astronomer, 1902

A man has been arrested in New York for attempting to extort funds from ignorant and superstitious people by exhibiting a device, which he says will convey the human voice any distance over metallic wires so that it will be heard by the listener at the other end. He calls this instrument a telephone. Well-informed people know that it is impossible to transmit the human voice over wires.
—News item in a New York newspaper, 1868

TWO PATHS TO PAIN

As we've discovered, there are two ways for humanity
to experience pain:

1. Path of the Ego—the physical pain of the body
   and our emotional being
2. Path of the Soul—the spiritual pain of the
   shattering of one's ego

Each of us is given a choice: Which pain do we want to
experience? Both forms of pain will bring the ultimate
result—the perfection of the world, paradise, and the
infinite fulfillment of every conceivable human desire
for eternity. Both paths will awaken our desire and
appreciation for the Light of the Creator.

So what's the problem? We've been trekking the path
that is, without question, the more cumbersome, difficult, and painful of our two choices. We have been
choosing the Path of the Ego, the path of unimaginable
pain, for thousands of years. And it's been working. You

can be sure that a desire for relief from all suffering is reaching near-saturation levels after all these centuries of pain. We are all ready for a change, or at least a break. So it's time to take a breath, reassess our situation, and . . .

CHOOSE THE OTHER ROUTE!

If we just choose the second path, the Path of the Soul, where only our ego suffers, life will be fulfilling and unimaginably joyful as we evolve along the way to our ultimate destination.

THE DYNAMICS OF PAIN AND PLEASURE

When the ego is in control, strong and healthy, you and I have absolutely no awareness or appreciation of true happiness and authentic fulfillment. We wind up settling for the lowest forms of pleasure that gratify only the ego. Why do you think people fall into the grip of addictions? Addiction to alcohol, food, sex, and shopping (just to name a few) are easy ways to temporarily satisfy the ego's hunger for pleasure. And, naturally enough, the ego makes you feel that you're a winner when you indulge. But you aren't. You just think you are.

If you find yourself barking up the same tree again and again with no gain to show for it, it's time to take a closer look at the tree. What, specifically, are the pleasures that your ego seeks to soothe itself? You don't have to tell me. I already know. The fixes our ego craves fall into one category:

Anything money can buy.

Possessions. Vacations. Food. Drink. Drugs. All the things that give you a bit of pleasure-inducing bang for your buck but leave you feeling empty—and looking for more before you know it.

But there is another way. There is another watering hole where the depth and purity of the refreshing waters are infinite and immensely satisfying. How do you find this place? You find it by waging war against your ego, and resisting its lower forms of pleasure. Yes, you will experience momentary pain when you do so, but then you'll acquire the lasting fulfillment I'm talking about—pleasure in its highest form.

What is that specifically? It's the opposite of the low-end pleasures toward which we gravitate. The highest forms of pleasure also fit into one broad category:

Everything that money <u>cannot</u> buy.

Love. Respect. Integrity. Serenity. Bliss. Satisfaction. You get the picture. All of these things already belong to you. Yes, they are yours. But your ego has made you forget that all-important fact. Your ego has prompted you again and again to override your divine essence, which is nothing short of a slice of heaven.

OUT OF TOUCH

We have no idea any more what true fulfillment really is. Everything that falls in this second category actually seems foreign to us. When the ego is in control (which is 99% of the time), we fail to recognize what authentic fulfillment is. We can hardly recall what it means. Our taste buds don't even recognize it when it rests on our tongue.

Moreover, it seems we don't want true fulfillment. Sure, everyone will say they want peace of mind, quality relationships, a soul mate, and good health. But in truth, all too often the choices we make do not bring us these things, so we must not really want them. *Why not?* Because we allow the ego's incessant broadcasts to run our lives. And the ego despises true fulfillment. The ego detests anything and everything that is associated with the Light, for darkness allows the ego to flourish. The ego is constantly looking for ways to undermine your authentic self, my authentic self, and the authentic purpose of humanity—ultimate fulfillment.

For instance, the real you desires good health. But the ego wants ice cream, chips, bacon, candy, and all kinds of junk food. Why? It's simple. The ego wants to keep you overweight, isolated, and in pain. In other words, it's the Adversary who is controlling your thoughts and desires. So, what can you do? Read this part carefully (and more than once).

The only way to get in touch with your essential self and your true desires is to identify the ego.

When you do, when the ego is unmasked, then, and only then, can you make room to genuinely desire and appreciate real fulfillment.

Let's say that you work sixty hours a week—for the sake of your family, you tell yourself. Such a lifestyle can only cause a great deal of heartache to you and your family. But the moment you recognize the ego's influence on your choices, your impulse to work yourself to an early grave weakens, and you begin to see the appeal of spending more quality time with your spouse and kids.

Now that's really making a difference for the sake of your family. And for your own sake, too! Get it?

By defeating the ego, you establish contact with the real you and thereby connect with the true desires in your soul.

But you know the drill by now. The ego won't go down without a fight. It creates fearful fantasies in an attempt to get you to surrender.

If I work less, I'll lose that promotion I've been promised. I couldn't take that.

I can't afford to take time off. We've got too many bills right now.

What value would I have without my career?

I have to work overtime to make up for my failures as a partner and parent.

Now these are pretty painful thoughts. The ego uses tactics like this every time you try to recognize it. Or provoke it. Or eradicate it.

In order to help all humankind overthrow the ego once and for all, its wisest students of life and spirit have provided us with an ancient, yet state-of-the-art technology known as Kabbalah. These veteran warriors and this time-tested technology stand ready to help us at all times.

THE POWER OF CHOICE

Being a warrior and using this technology means making a life-altering choice every day, every hour, and every minute. You can choose an egocentric response or a soul response to every situation you face in life. What does this mean on a practical level?

The Egocentric Response

An egocentric response means we react. Period. When we react without thinking to people and events around us, it's our ego that's steering the ship. Here are some examples:

- Someone hurts our feelings and we react with anger.
- Someone makes more money than we do and we react with envy.
- We make a lot of money in a deal and we react with happiness.

See the pattern here? Something outside of us—something external—is inciting a reaction by our ego.

Good or bad, happy or sad, in either case we are reacting. The problem is that this stance gives us no control. Zero. The ego is in control. Completely. And the ego swings wildly from happiness to depression as it responds to external stimulation of every kind. Good news. Bad news. It doesn't matter. What does matter is that choosing to react in this manner always keeps us the furthest from the Light of the Creator. It might offer our ego momentary gratification, but our body and soul will pay the price with nonstop pain.

There's an old saying: *You must have a genuine belief in God in order to serve God. But you don't have to believe in the devil in order to serve the devil.*
Think about it. Your egocentric reactions serve Satan whether you're aware of this fact or not, and serving Satan is a surefire path to perpetual pain and chaos.

The Soul Response

There is another way to respond. Remember that we always have a choice, and when we're willing to take a hit of momentary pain for our long-term good we're choosing the Soul Response. When we respond in alignment with our true authentic essence, our soul, we are no longer reactive.

We are proactive.

We are not reacting to things around us. Instead, we are in **control**. We are the **cause** of our own happiness and state of mind. We are the **creator** of the events in our life. We are the director of our movie.

How is this accomplished? The key lies in what kabbalists call **Resistance**. A Soul Response means that instead of responding to our ego's promptings, we resist our instinctive reaction and stop for a moment. In that pause, we recognize that our ego is trying to control us. In other words, we see that the person in front of us (or the circumstances in which we find ourselves)

is not the true cause of our distress. These external stimuli are merely triggering our ego to protest-loudly.

In this moment, we can elect to **resist** the impulse to act. We do this by:

- Admitting to ourselves that the ego is flaring up right now.
- Releasing ourselves from the impulsive responses flooding our body.
- Accepting the momentary sting.
- And allowing the Light to fill us.

The moment we do this, our external antagonists disappear. They cease being antagonists at all. We witness miracles. We see transformation in everyone around us—friend and foe. We experience positive changes we never believed possible. But don't just take my word for it. Try it. Test it. Observe what happens to your perceived enemies when you start looking at them as your teammates (and soul mates) and you start recognizing the Adversary/Ego, seeing him as the enemy to be defeated.

Now here's the amazing part: even if we fail for a moment and find ourselves in the throes of a reactive fit, the very fact that we are aware that it is our ego at work—that we can admit it, confess it, own up to it, and acknowledge it—is 99% of the battle! Now we are waging war like a true kabbalist.

You can be sure that admitting you have an ego in any situation is excruciatingly painful. It is so painful that most of the world will never even try it. That's because what most people don't consciously know is that resistance hurts for but a moment, but it never causes lasting harm. On the contrary, it is the gateway to Heaven on Earth.

THE FINAL STEP

Now that you have connected to the Light of the Creator by practicing Resistance, *all* things are possible—including taking the most important step in expunging the ego. That step is **Sharing**. By resisting the ego, you've become a vessel for God's Light, which you now can share with others. Sharing is the only way. You have to give the Light away in order to keep the Light burning inside of you. By giving you receive release from your own pain, and make possible the release of pain for others.

How is this possible? When you are giving selflessly to another person, you are literally without SELF (without ego), and in this state you transcend the pain that plagues human existence. Selfless sharing and pain simply cannot coexist.

So how do we go about the business of sharing? There is an infinite number of ways to share Light. In that moment when the ego is without voice or influence, you will know the best way to reveal God's Light and release pain. Maybe you'll reach out and place a comforting hand on your spouse's shoulder. Maybe you'll slow down to let the car behind you pass instead of speeding up or stepping on the brakes. Maybe you'll tell your parents—or your children—that you love them, instead of trying to convince them that your way is best. These are all ways of sharing Light. And these few examples are just the beginning. The ways in which we can reveal God's love are endless. I bet you can even think of a few right now.

When you share your Light, you choose selflessness over selfishness.

You choose, "What can I do to assist this other person?" over "What's in it for me?"

You choose your soul over your ego. By doing so, you choose the gift of physical and spiritual well-being over pain.

DECONSTRUCTING CHOICE

What we have discussed throughout this book regarding the nature of pain, pleasure, and achieving lasting fulfillment can be illustrated most succinctly in what kabbalists call the Three Column System.

In a nutshell, the Three Column System refers to these three concepts:

1. The temporary PLEASURE that comes with gratifying the ego.
2. Our DESIRE for this temporary pleasure.
3. Our free will to RESIST the temporary pleasure of the ego and instead fulfill the longings of our soul.

People who merely react to their ego and accept its pursuit of pleasure are living life according to a Two Column System.

1. Their ego desires pleasure.
2. They take the pleasure.

But we understand now that the Two Column System ultimately leaves our soul mired in pain. Thankfully, we have been given the power to choose which system will rule our lives. And we can choose the Three Column System, in which free will is the essential third component.

Temporary   Egocentric
Pleasure   Desire for Pleasure

Free Will
To Resist Ego

By using our free will to defy the ego and reveal Light we can abolish pain and create lasting pleasure (not the temporary kind that leaves us aching and empty). Fortunately, the technology of Kabbalah is a tool that offers us the strength, wisdom, and power to choose the higher ground and resist the ego, to share Light and release the grip of lasting pain.

CHOOSE THE PAIN TO LOSE THE PAIN

Whoa! Ouch! That stings. It burns! I don't want to let go of my opinion. It hurts to let it go. I've got to have the last word. It would be so much easier to blame the other person in order to ease this pressure and feel a bit of pleasure instead.

This is the voice of your ego. It will hurt you to admit it. It will ache to acknowledge it. It will be agonizing to just let it go. But the agony and pain will be momentary. Temporary. Brief. It will pass. Embracing the pain allows you to transcend it. In other words, when you choose the pain, you lose the pain. That's the paradox. The ego will take the pain for you! Magically. Suddenly your soul has been unleashed. The real you will emerge. Another battle is won.

With more resilience and determination than ever before, you will move on to face the next battle in the war against the oldest enemy known to man. But these battles won't last forever. When enough battles are won, when a critical mass and threshold of victories are achieved, the war will be over for good. Suffering and pain will be obliterated forever. Paradise, beyond any joy or bliss your mind can conceive, will be yours for the savoring. You'll be home again.

MORE FROM NATIONAL BEST-SELLING AUTHOR YEHUDA BERG

Rebooting: Defeating Depression with the Power of Kabbalah

An estimated 18 million people in the United States suffer from depression—that's almost 10% of the population. So chances are good that you have, or someone you know has, been affected by it. Antidepressants, counseling, herbal remedies—all have been known to help treat the symptoms, but sometimes they fall short. If only you could click on the "Restart" button and get your internal software back on track. Now, in *Rebooting*, noted kabbalistic scholar and author Yehuda Berg shows how you can do just that by reconnecting with desire and light to emerge from this debilitating darkness.

THE TECHNOLOGY FOR THE SOUL™ SERIES

Beyond Blame: A Full-Responsibility Approach to Life

If you think that chaos and suffering in your life is random or caused by external circumstances, think again! It's time to take personal responsibility for life's problems rather than give in to the tendency to blame others for them. In this book, you'll find simple, practical tools to help you overcome this negative tendency and live a happier, more productive life. Learn how to eliminate "victim consciousness" and improve your life, starting today.

The Monster is Real: How to Face Your Fears and Eliminate Them Forever

Admit it—at this very moment, you're afraid of something, or maybe even lots of things. This book shows you how to attack and defeat your fears at their most basic level. It offers practical kabbalistic tools for eliminating fear at its source so you can begin to live life to its fullest extent.

The Dreams Book: Finding Your Way in the Dark

Lift the curtain of reality and discover the secrets of dream interpretation that have remained hidden for centuries. Learn powerful techniques to attract soul mates, improve relationships, recognize career opportunities, and much more. This book holds the key to navigating the dreamscape, where the answers to life's questions are revealed.

God Does Not Create Miracles, You Do!

Stop waiting for a miracle and start making miracles happen! Discover powerful tools to help you break free of whatever is standing between you and the complete happiness you deserve. This book gives you the formula for creating the connection with the true source of miracles that lies only within yourself.

Kabbalah on Love

This charming little book has a simple yet profound message: Love is not something you learn or acquire but an essence within, waiting to be revealed. Buried by layers of ego, fear, shame, doubt, low self-esteem, and other limitations, the incredibly powerful force that is love can only be activated by sharing and serving unconditionally. Only then will the layers fall away and the essence of love reveal itself. The book draws the distinction between love and need, which is a selfish product of ego, and reminds us that we cannot love someone else until we figure out how to love ourselves and connect with the love within.

The Red String Book: The Power of Protection

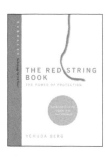

Discover the ancient wisdom behind the popularity of the Red String—the timeless technology known as Kabbalah. Worn on the left wrist, an authentic Red String provides protection against the "Evil Eye"—all negative effects that exist in the world. In *The Red String Book*, Yehuda Berg reveals how everyone can learn to use this simple yet effective tool for self-defense and healing.

The Power of Kabbalah

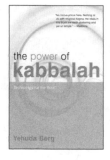

Imagine your life filled with unending joy, purpose, and contentment. Imagine your days infused with pure insight and energy. This is *The Power of Kabbalah*. It is the path from the momentary pleasure that most of us settle for, to the lasting fulfillment that is yours to claim. Your deepest desires are waiting to be realized. Find out how, in this basic introduction to the ancient wisdom of Kabbalah.

Also available: *The Power of Kabbalah Card Deck*

MORE PRODUCTS THAT CAN HELP YOU BRING THE WISDOM OF KABBALAH INTO YOUR LIFE

The Secret: Unlocking the Source of Joy & Fulfillment
By Michael Berg

The Secret reveals the essence of life in its most concise and powerful form. Several years before the latest "Secret" phenomenon, Michael Berg shared the amazing truths of the world's oldest spiritual wisdom in this book. In it, he has pieced together an ancient puzzle to show that our common understanding of life's purpose is actually backwards, and that anything less than complete joy and fulfillment can be changed by correcting this misperception.

God Wears Lipstick: Kabbalah for Women
By Karen Berg

For thousands of years, women were banned from studying Kabbalah, the ancient source of wisdom that explains who we are and what our purpose is in this universe. Karen Berg changed that. She opened the doors of The Kabbalah Centre to all who would seek to learn.

In *God Wears Lipstick*, Karen Berg shares the wisdom of Kabbalah, especially as it affects you and your relationships. She reveals a woman's special place in the universe and why women have a spiritual advantage over men. She explains how to find your soulmate and your purpose in life, and empowers you to become a better human being.

Also available: God Wears Lipstick Card Deck

Secrets of the Zohar: Stories and Meditations to Awaken the Heart
By Michael Berg

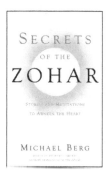

The *Zohar*'s secrets are the secrets of the Bible, passed on as oral tradition and then recorded as a sacred text that remained hidden for thousands of years. They have never been revealed quite as they are here in these pages, which decipher the codes behind the best stories of the ancient sages and offer a special meditation for each one. Entire portions of the *Zohar* are presented, with the Aramaic and its English translation in side-by-side columns. This allows you to scan and to read aloud so that you can draw on the *Zohar*'s full energy and achieve spiritual transformation. Open this book and open your heart to the Light of the *Zohar*!

Immortality: The Inevitability of Eternal Life
By Rav Berg

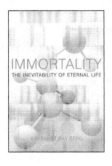

This book will totally change the way in which you perceive the world, if you simply approach its contents with an open mind and an open heart.

Most people have it backwards, dreading and battling what they see as the inevitability of aging and death. But, according to the great Kabbalist Rav Berg and the ancient wisdom of Kabbalah, it is eternal life that is inevitable.

With a radical shift in our cosmic awareness and the transformation of the collective consciousness that will follow, we can bring about the demise of the death force once and for all—in this "lifetime."

THE ZOHAR

Composed more than 2,000 years ago, the *Zohar* is a set of 23 books, a commentary on biblical and spiritual matters in the form of conversations among spiritual masters. But to describe the *Zohar* only in physical terms is greatly misleading. In truth, the *Zohar* is nothing less than a powerful tool for achieving the most important purposes of our lives. It was given to all humankind by the Creator to bring us protection, to connect us with the Creator's Light, and ultimately to fulfill our birthright of true spiritual transformation.

More than eighty years ago, when The Kabbalah Centre was founded, the *Zohar* had virtually disappeared from the world. Few people in the general population had ever heard of it. Whoever sought to read it—in any country, in any language, at any price—faced a long and futile search.

Today all this has changed. Through the work of The Kabbalah Centre and the editorial efforts of Michael Berg, the *Zohar* is now being brought to the world, not only in the original Aramaic language but also in English. The new English *Zohar* provides everything for connecting to this sacred text on all levels: the original Aramaic text for scanning; an English translation; and clear, concise commentary for study and learning.

THE KABBALAH CENTRE

The International Leader in the Education of Kabbalah

Since its founding, The Kabbalah Centre has had a single mission: to improve and transform people's lives by bringing the power and wisdom of Kabbalah to all who wish to partake of it.

Through the lifelong efforts of Kabbalists Rav and Karen Berg, and the great spiritual lineage of which they are a part, an astonishing 3.5 million people around the world have already been touched by the powerful teachings of Kabbalah. And each year, the numbers are growing!

• • • •

If you were inspired by this book in any way and would like to know how you can continue to enrich your life through the wisdom of Kabbalah, here is what you can do next:

Call 1-800-KABBALAH where trained instructors are available 18 hours a day. These dedicated people are willing to answer any and all questions about Kabbalah and help guide you along in your effort to learn more.

This book is dedicated to our parents,

Judy Parrott

and

John and Carol De Chaud

Thank you for your light, your love, your wisdom,
and your encouragement.

We couldn't have picked better parents.

With Love,

Frank and Annette Wolf